SECRETS

The Benefits Of Being Discreet

REV. DR. WILLIAM OBENG-DARKO

CIBUNET
Publishing

SECRETS – The Benefits of Being Discreet

Secrets – The Benefits of Being Discreet
By Rev. Dr. William Obeng-Darko

Printed in the United States of America
Second Edition

ISBN: 10: 1-940260-01-9
ISBN: 13: 978-1-940260-01-3

Unless otherwise indicated, Bible quotations are taken from the New King James Bible & King James Bible. Copyright © 2014

Cover Design By: Faith Walley

Published By:
Cibunet Publishing
P. O. Box 444
Woodlawn, NY 10470
Email: admin@cibunet.com
Website: www.cibunet.com

CONTENTS

ACKNOWLEDGMENT

I give thanks to God, whom I serve and whose I am for His continuous inspiration and the gifts in my life to serve my generation.

I also appreciate my family and friends who always encouraged me to put my teachings into writings.

To my publishers CIBUNET who worked day and night to make this project a reality, I am grateful.

FOREWORD

"Take hold of instruction: let her not go; keep her; for she is your life"

Books are written for different purposes, some for reading pleasure, while others are for general information. However this book in your hand is written for the purpose of instruction in the way of life. The contents are meant to open your eyes to light and bless you with wisdom. Read them over and over again, till the truths are established as a new order of your life. Keep this book. You may have to continue making reference to it as a guide, as your climb the ladder of life and success

May you succeed where many have faltered.

William Obeng-Darko

SECRETS – The Benefits of Being Discreet

Chapter One

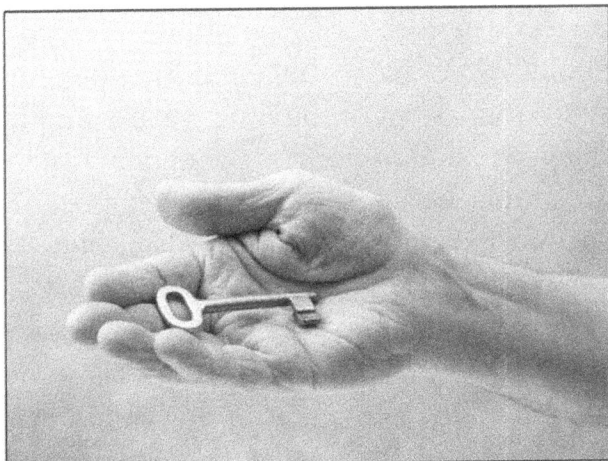

GOD HAS SECRETS

O ne of the greatest blessings of our existence as human beings, is the opportunity to have relationships with the people in our world, which enables us fellowship with one another. Whether as married couples, family relations, friends, acquaintances, co-workers or business colleagues, our relationships allow us to celebrate our successes and inspire one another to do great things. Alongside the benefits of relationships also comes envy. Envy is an evil vice that can sometimes become very destructive to great relationships. It is important that we limit potential manifestations of envy that could hinder our progress in life. Jesus said in Matthew 10:36 that "A man's enemies will be those of his own household." We have the enemy within and the enemy without. Most of the time we are afraid of the enemy outside, but rather it is the enemy from within that we should be concerned about. It is the enemy from within that takes information out. The enemy from within can paint you as dirty and it will stick because everyone knows that they have access to the information they provide about you. It is sometimes inconceivable, but siblings from the same household can be envious of each other, your spouse or best friend can be jealous of you. Even though you may have heard of such scenarios and you are aware of the possibility, most often you think it may never happen to you and so you do not embrace this reality in your life. Several principles in God's word point to this reality including the fact that God is careful with how He disseminates information to us as human beings.

Deuteronomy 29:29 reads, "The secret things belong to the LORD our God, but those things which are revealed belong to us and to our children forever, that we may do all the words of this law"

God has secrets. The word 'secret' means 'hidden'. There are secrets that belong to God. This scripture talks about two things. Firstly, it talks about things that are revealed and secondly, things that are kept from being revealed. It talks about the secret things of God. God has secrets that are hidden from everyone. Only the Father knows such information. There are also other things that are revealed. The things that are revealed are the things that he has told us. If you do not tell people your business they will never get to know them. But in dealing with the Father, the Father has revealed certain things to us. It does not mean that what we know is all that there is to be told or said. No! There is so much that God has not revealed to us because they do not belong to us. The Bible says "they do not belong unto us." God has told us the things that belong to us. But there are things that do not belong to us. The question is what are we going to do with such information? They are for God. We have to ask ourselves this question anytime we want to share something with someone. Is this information for this person? What will the person do with the information I am providing them with?

Sometimes we give out information that has destroyed the lives of other people. When certain information gets into the hands of some people, it gives them sleepless nights. They begin to plan and plot on how to hinder others from making progress and taking hold of things that rightfully belongs to them. How did he or she get that knowledge? It is because you told them. God always looks at the things that belong to us and He tells us about them because He wants us to do something about a situation or to be forewarned of an impending danger. The knowledge, vision, dream or word that God gives to us, belongs to us and our children, so that we will know His will and plans for our lives and be compliant with His commandments. God does not tell us things without a reason. God tells us because there is a purpose, which is that He wants us to obey his Word. He wants us to become doers and that is why He tells us things. When God reveals something to you, it is because he wants you to do something about it. Most of the time, He wants you to pray about it. He did not show it to you just for the fun of it.

We have to learn from the Father. He decides what information to share with us and the information He must keep away from us. This is not because He does not love us, but it is for our own good and protection. If we knew the number of dangers that

God protects and delivers us from, we will walk in constant fear. The Bible talks about the destruction that takes place in the noonday and the arrow that flies by night as the only details we have of unseen demonic activity that shrouds our lives. But we always go in and out and are safe because of the power of God that protects and keeps us from harm. The example we learn from our heavenly Father is to ask ourselves; "Does he or she need to know this? Did God tell me this for my ears or heart only? How can I determine that this information belongs to this other person? What will he or she do with that? Do I have to give information for the sake of it?

Nations have what we call 'classified information'. These nations cannot give such information out because that can be detrimental to the nation. Businesses and organizations also have classified information. It is only believers that do not have classified information. Most of the time in talking too much, we end up giving out too much information. A friend calls and within five minutes we have given information that should have taken us ten years to give. Then we wonder why some things did not go well and there seems to be unwarranted opposition to what we do. We wonder why someone who used to be a friend has suddenly withdrawn from us. It is simply because we talk too much.

When God tells us some things, He does not tell us for conversation sake. God gives us information because He wants us to become doers of His word. My question to you is: "Do you have any classified information"? Or do you not consider anything as classified as far as you are concerned? Do you know that information is very costly and expensive to gain? Nations pay a lot of money for spies to gather information for them. People go undercover to get information. In the food industry, some companies keep their recipes, formulas and trade secrets as classified information. For example companies like Coca-Cola and Pepsi have formulas for creating their soft drinks, which they keep as a secret from each other. You can work there for many years and yet you will never know their formula. There are some restaurants where the food they serve is prepared in a semi-finished state before it is brought in for finishing at the in-house kitchen of the restaurant. Otherwise the employees will take all the secrets of the company with them to start their own restaurants. Recently I was in a restaurant, and I let them know I wanted a low sodium diet and they informed me that the food was prepared at another location and brought in, so they could not do much about my request.

Most often, we do not consider ourselves as worth having classified information. Whenever something happens, we call people to inform them even when that will not profit them but rather stir up envy and jealousy. Just think about a business like the Coca Cola Company that has guarded their secret formula for the 'coke' drink for several years. You cannot walk up to their corporate offices and ask them for this secret formula and expect them to give it to you. Companies are always on the lookout for fresh competitors and they will do everything within their power to hide information that gives away their trade secrets.

Most often, we associate keeping secrets with evil schemes. We think that if it is a secret, then we have something to hide, which is bad and evil. Keeping secrets is not evil, it is the content of what you are keeping that determines if it is evil or not. As an organization, you must know that if certain trade secrets or information gets into the hands of some people it is just going to stir up unnecessary competition. Someone may rise up and challenge you to an unnecessary competition. Such a potential competitor will now devise ways to overtake you as a result of information they got hold of.

"Now after Jesus was born in Bethlehem of Judea in the days of Herod the king, behold, wise men from the East came to Jerusalem, saying, "Where is He who has been born King of the Jews? For we have seen His star in the East and have come to worship Him." When Herod the king heard this, he was troubled, and all Jerusalem with him. And when he had gathered all the chief priests and scribes of the people together, he inquired of them where the Christ was to be born. So they said to him, "In Bethlehem of Judea, for thus it is written by the prophet:'But you, Bethlehem, in the land of Judah, Are not the least among the rulers of Judah; For out of you shall come a Ruler Who will shepherd My people Israel.'" Then Herod, when he had secretly called the wise men, determined from them what time the star appeared. And he sent them to Bethlehem and said, "Go and search carefully for the young Child, and when you have found Him, bring back word to me, that I may come and worship Him also." When they heard the king, they departed; and behold, the star which they had seen in the East went before them, till it came and stood over where the young Child was. When they saw the star, they rejoiced with exceedingly great joy. And when they had come into the house, they saw the young Child with Mary His mother, and fell down and worshiped Him. And when they had opened their treasures, they presented gifts to Him: gold, frankincense, and myrrh. Then, being divinely warned in a dream that they should not return to Herod, they departed for their own country another way"

Matthew 2:1-12

At the time Jesus Christ was born, the scripture records of wise men from the east that had seen the star of Jesus and followed it to Israel. When they arrived they went to the ruler named 'King Herod' to inform him about the star of a new born king that was apparent in the sky. King Herod was disturbed by the news of a potential competition to his reign over the Israelites and so he had to devise a way to kill the baby Jesus. The only reason King Herod devised such a devious plan was because the wise men had innocently revealed God's secrets to him. If God wanted Herod to know about Jesus, He would have told Herod directly. The wise men from the east saw the star, they had the right interpretation of the meaning of the star and they followed it. Instead of continuing to follow the star, they went to King Herod's palace to go find out. King Herod had not been told by God, so he did not know. The bible says he had to call in the Jewish leaders to ask them if it was recorded in their books where a king was to be born. They confirmed a king will be born in Bethlehem of Judea but had no further details. King Herod instructed the wise men to go and look for the baby and when they find him, to bring him word so that he may also go and worship him. That is what we call 'politically correct' words. People learn to use politically correct words in most cases to hide their ulterior motives.

19

When most people tell you they are standing with you so you should divulge information for them to pray effectively for you, it is a lie! They may be lying and will not be praying for you. Most likely they will take up your idea or sell it to others. Sometimes people will ask you, "What is up with you? Then you tell them your new venture of importing goods from China. Then they say in their minds; "wow, if that is the new way people are making money, then I will not be left out". So they immediately start to make plans to also start importing from China or they will find a way to discourage you. Herod was politically correct in how he stated his position concerning the potential competitor for the throne of Israel. You would think that Herod was a good man because he said he also wanted to go and worship the child. But his real motive was that he was looking for a way to kill the baby before he grows up to compete with him for the throne. We do not know what is in a man's heart so we cannot judge people only on the basis of their 'politically correct' words.

The wise men were disappointed because they did not get any help from Herod. But then when they came out of his palace, the star was still there. They continued following it until they found the manger where Jesus was born. We have to follow the star. We have to follow the Holy Spirit. Do not go telling your secrets to people. If these wise men had followed the star diligently without deviating to seek man's help, King Herod would never have known about their mission. The angel of the Lord had to appear in a dream to warn the wise men and say to them "do not go back the same way that you came, do not go to Herod, get up and depart." The angel warned them because they were going back to tell Herod they had found the baby Jesus. Because the wise men had given out information about the birth of Jesus to the wrong person, King Herod, God had to send His angel to instruct Joseph the earthly father of Jesus in a dream in Matthew 2:13-18.

"Now when they had departed, behold, an angel of the Lord appeared to Joseph in a dream, saying, "Arise, take the young Child and His mother, flee to Egypt, and stay there until I bring you word; for Herod will seek the young Child to destroy Him."
When he arose, he took the young Child and His mother by night and departed for Egypt, and was there until the death of Herod, that it might be fulfilled which was spoken by the Lord through the prophet, saying, "Out of Egypt I called My Son." Then Herod, when he saw that he was deceived by the wise men, was exceedingly angry; and he sent forth and put to death all the male children who were in Bethlehem and in all its districts, from two years old and under, according to the time which he had determined from the wise

men. Then was fulfilled what was spoken by Jeremiah the prophet, saying: "A voice was heard in Ramah, Lamentation, weeping, and great mourning, Rachel weeping for her children, Refusing to be comforted, Because they are no more"

The angel told Joseph to stay in Egypt and not make any attempt to move out, "Arise, take the young Child and His mother, flee to Egypt, and stay there until I bring you word; for Herod will seek the young Child to destroy Him." Joseph and Mary took the child and went to stay in Egypt. After Herod had waited for a year or two he ordered that babies two years old should be killed. Do you see how parents who had babies in that category lost their children simply because somebody went and told something they should not have told? When God says something to you, it does not belong to other people, you have to keep it to yourself. If you want to share it with somebody pray about it and be convinced in your heart that God wants you to share that with the person.

I remember sometime in the past there was an incident that had occurred that I was so desirous of sharing with someone I considered a very good friend. But when I called and I began to speak to her, I begun to experience a 'check' in my heart and it was like my spirit kept saying "stop speaking, do not share that with her". Only to find out some months later that the person I had always thought of as a friend did not actually have my interest at heart. This person was very envious and jealous of me and I had no idea. Be careful with those you share your secrets with. When they do not rejoice with you when things seem to be going on well for you, this is a red flag. You have to watch all these things.

It is very important that we know what belongs to us and what belongs to other people. This is wisdom from God. Do not be afraid that you have access to classified information. God has classified information also. It can cost you a lot when you divulge information that you do not have to. Sometimes things have to mature. You have to feel comfortable, that for a season some information must remain with you. This belongs to me and I am not going to send it out.

God bless you, God keep you, God speak to your heart, God direct your footsteps and God show you what to say and what not to say. May you receive inner strength to keep what must be kept as a secret until the right time in the precious name of Jesus Christ.

SECRETS – The Benefits of Being Discreet

Chapter Two

PROTECT YOUR RIGHTS OF PRIVACY

I t is important to always remember that though some information may be useful to the public, some others are private. When you do not make that differentiation and you give out all information, your enemies can use it to hurt you. It could potentially stir up envy and competitive jealousy. When people get into competition with us, it sometimes orchestrates bad projections. People begin to project things in their minds against our wellbeing. Some may pretend to love us in order to hide their evil motives. It hurts them because we are making progress in certain areas of our lives where they may feel stagnated.

I notice that most often people are wise until they become Christians, then they change their ways to become careless. They do not operate in an intelligent manner because they develop the notion that as a Christian nobody can harm them. Well, the reality is that someone can harm you when you are careless. A car may run into you on the road, when you are careless and do not watch where you are going. It is therefore important for us to be intelligent and operate in wisdom.

Owing to the manner in which some people were raised from childhood, they become naturally trusting of almost everyone around them. As a result, keeping a secret may sound bad since people may consider you an evil person. They think that as a Christian you should not have a secret. It is often commonly said that if you are hiding it, then it has to be evil. It is not only evil that we hide, we hide good things too. Good must be hidden at times. Can you imagine that on some occasions, after healing some folk Jesus instructed them: "do not tell anybody about it". Why would he hide that? Was that evil? No! You see if you do not read the scriptures with insight you can become very careless, you will lack intelligence and your heart will act in an unintelligent way.

"Therefore, when they had come together, they asked Him, saying, "Lord, will you at this time restore the kingdom to Israel?" And He said to them, "It is not for you to know the times or seasons which the Father has put in His own authority. But you shall receive power when the Holy Spirit has come upon you; and you shall be witnesses to Me in Jerusalem, and in all Judea and Samaria, and to the end of the earth"

Acts 1:6-8

Our Lord Jesus Christ had finished his assignment on earth and was about to ascend into heaven. He had to go back to the Father who sent him so he was preparing his disciples for his departure. In Acts 1:6 they ask Him: "Lord, will you at this time restore the kingdom to Israel?" Now this had been on their minds all the time. The Romans had colonized Israel and so the Israelites were under Roman domination.

The Jews were looking forward to the time when Israel will gain their political independence. The Jews knew that at some point, God was going to restore Israel so that Israel would become a great nation once more. So they asked Jesus this question, "Lord, will you at this time restore the kingdom to Israel?" And He said to them, "It is not for you to know times or seasons which the Father has put in His own authority"

Now do you notice that there was some information they desired from Jesus? But the Lord said to them 'that is not for you to know'. It is not because someone asks you a question that you must give them an answer they are expecting. No! You do not have to do that. Jesus did not give them the answer. Jesus said to them, it is not for you to know. Do you know we have said things to people and they had no business knowing it? But we thought we were being Christian. We thought we were being nice. We thought we were being the children of God. Jesus was the savior of the world but he said to his disciples 'that is not for you to know'. Literally He was saying; 'it is not your business to know this'. Think about that and think about things we have said to people that they had no business knowing. Jesus said it is not for you to know what the Father has put in his own power. "The Father has put in his own power" simply means that it is the exclusive privilege of the

Father. The word 'power' there means 'right'. That is the Father's right, it is not for you, neither is it your right to know. We have rights and privileges. Jesus said; that is the Father's right and privileges, it is not for you to know. The times and the seasons appointed are of the Father but you must focus on your assignment. You will receive power when the Holy Ghost comes on you and that is what you must focus on. Jesus said to them, you go ahead and become witnesses, but as to when and how independence will come to Israel, that is the Father's privilege.

Some things are your rights. Do not let people intrude into what is your exclusive right. Do not let people make you feel like you do not have any rights so that they must have access to whatever they demand to know from you. Sometimes I ask people for some information and they say, "I cannot tell you", and I say "okay". It is their right and privilege. They have that liberty to do what they please. If something is your right, you have liberty to do as you please with it.

There are some of us who go about our business and yet everyone knows what we are doing. They know how we got what we got. They know what our next steps are going to be. They know our mindset and everything about us. Can you imagine? It means that we have no privacy anymore.

You may say: 'Oh he is my husband and so I have to tell him'. Then you quote the Bible and say "The two shall be one." Read the Bible carefully because sometimes we ignorantly add more words to the scriptures. The scripture says "The two shall be one flesh." There is a difference between becoming one mind and becoming one flesh. And the way you become one flesh is as a result of sexual intimacy. You are not even one flesh with your children even though that is your blood in them. It is the marriage union that produces one flesh. In fact it is not the entire marriage union but it is just sexual activity. The Bible says in 1 Corinthians 6:16, "Or do you not know that he who is joined to a harlot is one body with her? For "the two," He says, "shall become one flesh." Do not be ignorant and say "we are one flesh and so I have to tell him everything." No! Just because you are married does not mean you have lost your privileges and rights as a human being and as a wife or husband. You are not a slave. The fact that someone is your spouse does not mean you have to tell them everything. Where are your rights as an individual? There are some things that are exclusive rights to your husband. Just because you became a wife does not mean you are no more a woman. There are rights and privileges of a woman and that of a wife. You do not lose your rights as a woman by becoming a wife. We have put the wrong interpretation on the scripture that says "you have become one flesh." The Bible did not say you have become one. In fact if you are black and your wife is light skinned you do not become light skinned, you still remain black. You may say; 'We always have the same thoughts'. No! You cannot have the same thought, you are unique individuals and you are not the same. You were born to your parents and you have the DNA of your parents, your personality growing up, the school you went, your friends, your environment has all molded you. You may have married at the age of thirty and because you said "I do" during the declaration of your marriage vows and have engaged in sexual intercourse does not necessarily mean everything that you are and have been has changed, so that you are now the personality of your spouse. It does not work that way. You are still a distinct individual. Your rights have to be spelt out and respected.

Do you know that those who work in companies and even very big corporations do not have access to all information about the company? You do not have to know everything. There are some things that are classified as executive privileges. It is only those at the top of the leadership hierarchy that get to know such information. The leadership does not divulge all information to the whole work force.

When the police arrests you they tell you: 'you have a right to remain silent'. Just because they are asking you questions do not mean you answer them and give out everything information. You cannot tell your lawyer you divulged information to the police just because they were asking you questions. Your lawyer will tell you why you should not have answered their questions, because you have rights! You have to know what your rights and privileges are.

Do you know that when you stand before the court, they tell you what your rights are? You have a right to be quiet. That is your right. Do not yield and concede your rights to another person by telling everything as if you are so helpless. If I do not tell him, he is going to think this or that way. Let people think whichever way they please when you refuse to inform them. We got to be strong. What do you think the disciples were thinking about Jesus? They must have thought; but we are your friends, we have been with you. Jesus confidently said to them, "that is not for you to know". I like that! "That is not for you to know". That means that this does not belong to you. What you are trying to find out is not for you to know. That is the Father's right and privilege. The times and the seasons are the Father's rights not yours.

Do you know that sometimes God gives us a vision that is private and we carelessly go about sharing it with the public? It is exclusive and private, and we have a right to keep it. Get this wisdom. Several years ago I was in fasting and prayer and the Lord gave me a message. This is not something I had ever read or heard anybody teach about. This message dropped deep in my spirit. I wept when the Lord gave me that message. I said 'wow' because it was something that was going to help us, guide the future and how to remain in the Lord and much more. I was so excited and I wrote everything down as the Spirit of God was telling me as I knelt down before my chair. I had some good friends with whom I shared this message as brothers in Christ. Instead of being private about this message that God had given to me, I disclosed it to these friends. One day I was sitting with my friends and I said: "Ah do you know what the Lord just gave me a week ago?" They said, "What was it"? These were Holy Ghost filled, tongue speaking, faith and love preaching Ministers. And I revealed what God had told me in full detail. One of them asked me "Really, what Scriptures did God give you for this revelation?" I was so careless and just gave them the scriptures and how the Lord had explained them to me. I travelled and when I came back one of them had preached the message at Church and changed the title. He did not give me any credit for it. He preached it and turned it into a book, took the royalties and he is still enjoying that today. Because of that I cannot preach that message myself. Sometimes I go to places and I am going to preach and they tell me, 'I heard this preacher preach a message and it really blessed me'. Only to find out that it was my message, and sometimes I am tempted to say that was not his message. But I just keep quiet and say within me that it was my right but I yielded it because I was naïve and careless with a secret.

Most people hear others preach and go and preach the message without giving credit to those from who they heard it. They behave as though it was given to them directly from God. That is wrong, if you want to use someone's message, you have to call or write to them for permission to use the message or material.

Recently I visited one of my relatives and she was holding a book. I took the book, read it and it blessed me. I told her I was going to start a bible school very soon and I will need to use the book as one of the text books on prayer. I called the Pastor that wrote the book and told him his book was a blessing and requested to use it as a text book and quote from it. He agreed and so he sent me an official letter giving me the permission to use anything freely not only in that book but in all his books. That is the way we do it. You do not say the Lord gave me this message when the Lord did not give you that message. You already have begun on the premise of lies. That is why we have legal 'copyrights' over our creative rights and privileges.

Sometimes people come and ask you 'what is up with you? Then like a parrot you begin to tell them all your plans. We sometimes talk so fast that it is impossible to press the stop button when our conscience cautions us. We go on and on and we keep talking until we have sold out our secrets for nothing and invoked unnecessary competition.

I remember there was a group of young people who got hold of a huge amount of money. I do not know how they got it but they did not have ideas. They went around asking their friends what plans they had. Some people have ideas but they do not have money, while others have money but they lack ideas. These guys with money but no plans subtly got hold of the plans of some friends and executed it for themselves.

Sometimes you are not aware that your friends are simply scouting about and fishing for ideas. You carelessly tell them how God has opened a contact opportunity for you and in fact there is a certain man who is willing to help you. Why are you going into all those details? Is it their right to know? Sometimes you feel obliged because you think, he is my brother or because she is my sister or my friend. Do you know these same people may go behind you and do the same business with your contact person? By the time you go back to your contact he will tell you some guys sought his help and he has already made a commitment with the money that he would have used to help you. Those who were cheated off their contacts came before me and said; 'Pastor I do not think these guys are Christians'. They are Christians, just as much as you are, the only difference is you were naïve and became careless because you did not know what were your rights and privileges. You had the right to be silent but you chose to talk. There are many good hearted people who have fallen victims to these kind of schemes and tricks of people. The church world is not exempted and many Christians have become victims that are left wounded, bitter and cannot trust others again.

There is some information that only God knows. In Matthew 24:35&36 Jesus said, "Heaven and earth will pass away, but My words will by no means pass away. But of that day and hour no one knows, not even the angels of heaven, but My Father only." In fact if you read the entire Matthew chapter 24, Jesus

Christ was talking about the end of the world and His second coming. At times you will hear people say they predict a date that the world is coming to an end. These are all liars. The question is; "how did you know that? Only the Father knows, no one knows. People sell their stuff and give up on their careers, professions and work because they believe the world is coming to an end on a certain date. If you read the Bible you will realize that no man knows the day or the hour that the world is coming to an end. This is an exclusive right, it is only in the power of the Father.

Has the Father got secrets? Yes, they are hidden truths. Only the Father knows the time and the hour. He will call the Son and say to him now is the time to go. The hour, the minute, the month nobody knows. Forget about all these people who write books and say Jesus is coming at this time of the year. All these years came and went and still Jesus did not come. When we talk of the signs of his coming, yes, but when we begin to predict the date, time and hour and people go and stand on a mountain because they want to be the first to be caught up into the heavens; that is simply absurd. "But on that day and hour knows no man, no not the angels of heaven." Can you believe that the Father has kept it from the angels? They are with Him, worship Him daily and yet the Father keeps some secrets in Him without revealing it all. He could call Gabriel and say to angel Gabriel, 'I am actually planning to go in 3024. No! That is not for them to know. They are to carry on the job of worshipping and ministering, that is their assignment and leave God's privilege to be his privilege.

What is in your mind? Is there anything that sets you apart to say this is my right and privilege or you have allowed people to pull these things out of you? Do not allow people to read and predict you. Do not let them know your next move, do not be a lightweight as you go about your life goals. Nations train people to operate undercover so as to get information. Nations spend a lot of money to protect information. Industries and businesses have their exclusive rights and privileges. You cannot go to McDonalds and demand to know their recipes and how they make their various menus. Even the people who work there do not know. That is part of their trade secrets. Do you know people pay a lot to have part of that knowledge in order to operate as another McDonalds' franchise? You cannot have it free of charge. Imagine you go to a McDonalds and you begin to ask "Can you tell me what spices you use for your chickens because when I eat your burgers I feel so good". This is their business secret. That is what has set them apart. That is what is bringing money to them.

God wants to increase and bless us but these are some of the things that place us at a disadvantage. But we are not going to lose again. Let us be wise from this day forward. Honor and protect your rights and your privileges.

SECRETS – The Benefits of Being Discreet

Chapter Three

YOU MUST KEEP THINGS IN YOUR HEART

"It is the glory of God to conceal a thing but the honor of kings to search out a matter"

Proverbs 25:2

The word 'glory' there means 'goodness'. It is in the goodness of God to conceal a thing. However it is an honor to search it out. The word 'conceal' means to 'hide', to keep as a secret. God is the number one secret keeper; it is His glory to conceal a thing.

We read from Deuteronomy 29:29, "The secret things belong to the LORD our God, but those things which are revealed belong to us and to our children forever, that we may do all the words of this law." It is important to know what belongs to us and what does not, as well as what belongs to others and what does not. It is the responsibility of the king to search out a matter. Man is always investigating and finding out. There are people whose role is always to investigate and ask you questions. They always want to know. Just as the disciples asked Jesus, "Will you at this time restore the kingdom to Israel?" and Jesus told them it is not for you to know, yours is to receive power, yours is to go out there and preach the Gospel, which is your responsibility.

People do not feel it is wrong for them to find out things from you, they see it as an honor, it works to their advantage and to your disadvantage, so do not feel guilty to keep what belongs to you from others. We need to be confident and bold not to give out business secrets, our plans and any information that belong to our privacy.

At times people may not necessarily focus on what information belongs to them, but rather place upon themselves the burden of focusing on other people's matters. The book of 1 Thessalonians 4:11 reads, "That you also aspire to lead a quiet life, to mind your own business." Here the Apostle Paul talks about people busying themselves about other people's lives. They do not focus on their own business. People who do that are busybodies. There are people who do not feel at peace focusing on their own. Busybodies are not shy, and they do not lack boldness, they come in a crafty manner and sometimes pretend to care about you or others. They first volunteer information so you feel obligated to also respond with some information. They can be persistent when seeking information, some also pretend not to be interested in anything you have to say but then quietly absorb what you say. Keep things within you until the right time before you talk about them.

There are some revelations that God hid in the scriptures from generations past. God always has a right time to reveal or not to reveal information to mankind.

"How that by revelation He made known to me the mystery as I have briefly written already"

Ephesians 3:3

"The mystery which has been hidden from ages and from generations, but now has been revealed to His saints"

Colossians 1:26

The word 'hid' means 'kept secret', kept from others. The scripture says there are some truths which were hidden from generations and ages but now is being revealed to His saints. God could keep some truths for generations and for years. It is the honor of God to conceal a thing. We must learn this character of God, in order to know what to talk about and what not to talk about. There are divine reasons for keeping some revelation hidden until the right time. The problem is we have always emphasized on the negative side of keeping secrets. The general impression is that if you have a secret, then there is something devious about it for which reason you do not want anybody to know about it. Though that is the negative perception about secrets, there are many positive reasons for keeping certain information until they mature.

In Nehemiah 2:11&12 we read the story of some of the steps Nehemiah took in rebuilding the walls in

Jerusalem. "So I came to Jerusalem and was there three days. Then I arose in the night, I and a few men with me; I told no one what my God had put in my heart to do at Jerusalem; nor was there any animal with me, except the one on which I rode."

God placed some things in Nehemiah's heart and that was why he came from captivity. He asked permission from the king to come to Jerusalem because of the wall that was broken down. God placed something on his heart to do. What God placed on his heart to do was to go to Jerusalem to help rebuild the walls. But when he arrived, he says for three days or more he never told any man what God had put in his heart to do. God had placed some things on his heart but he kept them secret. He knew at what time to speak and at what time to keep quiet.

Most often we may make mention of a project or assignment that God has commissioned us to embark on. Those who hear us may either discount it jokingly or discourage us completely. After communing with God in prayer most people go about telling what God said to them. That is wrong. You have to keep it in your heart. At times you need to sit on some things for years. There are things I have sat on for one whole year. God just put it on my heart and I kept praying about it, thinking about it, looking and observing until the right time and I talked about it. Most of the information people around bring to me as a Pastor is what I already know about, but then I may act as though I am hearing it for the first time. Do not just be as talkative as a parrot. Most often God may not have even finished revealing the entire information and then we add our own words to complete the puzzle. No! God did not tell you so you go around saying it. That is why sometimes God cannot keep telling us some things. Nehemiah kept this in his heart. The Bible says that there is a time to be silent and there is a time to speak. There is a time when you keep these things in your heart. If your heart is not capable of keeping information, then it is important to pray for the Lord to enlarge your heart. It is due to the fact that some people have small hearts that they constantly spill over information through a leaking mouth to tell everybody.

Most often the reaction of people when you reveal what God said is like "are you sure God said this to you"? Do you not think that this is your mind? When they can ascertain your confidence about God being the source, then they either attempt to talk you out of it or they steal your word. As stealers of dreams, they go about peddling what you revealed from God to them as though God spoke to them.

Since God did not speak to them, they are thieves of the word.

"Is not My word like a fire?" says the Lord, "And like a hammer that breaks the rock in pieces? Therefore behold, I *am* against the prophets," says the LORD, "who steal My words everyone from his neighbor"

Jeremiah 23:29&30

These are stealers of the word. These people go around saying to people that God revealed certain things to them which often times is simply a peddling of what they heard from you. Some people do not have the decency to acknowledge that the Lord spoke to someone and I am happy to share that with you. That is common sense. Rather they come to you and say: "I was praying and the Lord spoke to me". But you know very well that they have not prayed. God said I am against those who steal my word. They cannot steal God's word from God that is why God said they steal God's word from one another.

When God speaks to your heart to embark on a certain career or start a business, it is not public information, so you do not have to go about broadcasting it. You must first conceal the matter in your heart and do some preliminary diligence. If God wanted the whole world to hear this information as a public matter, then He may have let it come forth as spontaneous prophecy at a public forum. Now God did not speak to the whole world about your new mission but He spoke to you in private so that is His word to you. Like Nehemiah you must first conceal it in your heart. You do not call your prayer partner on the phone and say "do you know these prayers we pray are very effective? Do you know the Lord spoke to me and said that I should get into car business, this thing has been on my heart and I really want to get into it and I do not even know how to start but I am going to trust God? This person listens to you and says "Praise the Lord, God is good."

The next time you see this person, they will say to you, "Praise the Lord, you know what; I want to also start a car business because God is speaking to my heart." God did not speak to them; they simply stole that word you got from God.

Such behavior and attitude of people is not a recent phenomenon as we discover in the book of Jeremiah where God said I am against them. I have seen it among clergy as well as among congregation members. People do not have the simple courtesy to say – "I got it from this person". It is best to always put it this way, 'Once we were in a camp meeting and a brother shared some revelation and it blessed me and I want to share it with you'. We would rather say that we got it from the last time we were praying and that we heard the Lord say it. When did the Lord say that to you? The Lord did not say that to you. God's word is like fire so we have to be careful. The previous verse says "Is not My word like fire." If God did not give it to you it will never burn in your heart. The fire of God's word will always burn in the heart of the one God spoke to. That word was for them, that word was spoken directly to them. God's word is like a hammer, it breaks rocks into pieces and it burns. So do not steal it because it is not going to burn in your heart and there will be no divine drive to orchestrate performance and prosperity.

At times we try to be good, but then when you share information before the due time, you have compromised what God wanted to do with you and through you. Prophets, prophetesses and seers must in some cases learn to keep their mouths shut. Most often they create more chaos than calm in the lives of people to whom they give personal revelations prematurely. Some people have the habit of asking after you have finished praying; "what is God is saying to you?" Is that your business? Is it God who is telling you to ask me what He is saying to me? If God wants to speak to you He will speak to you. Some would ask, "Pastor did you see something?" If I saw something do you think I am going to tell you, no I am not going to tell you. If God does not tell me to share it, I am not going to share it. Do not try to manipulate me to get things out of my mouth. People can steal God's word, God's vision, God's plan for your life if you keep sharing and sharing without limits. They will steal the plan and apply it for themselves. God says I am against them, but you are the one who volunteered that information. Nehemiah said "I did not say anything to any man of what God had put in my heart." Nehemiah carried it for many days and kept it without sharing it.

When God tells you to get into a venture, keep it in your heart and keep your mouth shut. Do you know the greatest secret keeper? Her name is Mary the mother of Jesus. No doubt that this was a young girl God could trust. Angels spoke to her, wise men spoke to her, prophets spoke to her but we do not have any record in the Bible that Mary shared those things that God spoke to her about?

Do you know it is not only God's vision for your life that people can steal? People can steal your ideas, even things you plan doing and people you plan marrying. I remember we were a group of friends and as you know, boys talk as well as girls. We were about five friends and were discussing about a young lady who was very beautiful. One of our friends said; "I really want to make a move on the lady" and we were in agreement and said, "Go ahead, you guys will be the perfect match", so we encouraged him. We with supported this friend and we encouraged him to gather the courage to speak to her. Do you know before this guy could make a move one of our friends who was part of the gathering had gone ahead and proposed to the lady? It was a shocker and the friend who first spoke his intentions said he was not going to give up because this was a sabotage of his intentions. But then this guy had sneaked behind him, just as anyone can overtake you on a journey while driving a car. When people do such things, it casts a shadow over your intentions. If the lady in this instance knew they were friends, then it will sound like a joke when both of them propose around the same time.

Some people are notorious hijackers who will always go ahead to take what belongs to you. Your place or position in life can be hijacked by others simply because you shared what you should have kept a secret. You know how someone takes what is yours, shares it publicly and then they take the glory that should have come to you. They take the glory and you are left with nothing.

Sometimes in life, God gives you one idea that could potentially lift you into wealth and prominence. If you do not value what God gives to you so as to move you up into prosperity, you may divulge it to thieves who may rise to occupy where you should be standing. They will not acknowledge you as the source of idea or the root to their success. The rest of the world may never get to know that this was an idea God gave you and it is you who should be standing on that platform of success. One good idea could be the basis for the advent of a great and prosperous business that rewards the owners in a big way monetarily. Unfortunately the owner of the idea may never get a dime out of the success because he revealed it ahead of time and lost any leverage or ownership to it. It is important to get wise, so that whenever anyone asks you about your plans, just say to them; 'I am still praying about it'. Let your plans remain in your heart for the simple fact that there is no other use of your plan except for them to copy it.

Though the scripture is clear that "It is God's glory to conceal a thing", our attitude generally is that if it is a good thing then it definitely must be shared, but if it is evil, then put it off the table. Do not put information on the table because it is good, rather keep it in your heart because everybody sitting there has an agenda. For some people, what you are sharing is going to stir up jealousy in their hearts against you. Others are thieves who will steal the idea and details from you. If the idea is about God's plan for your life they will definitely steal it. That is what goes on in the Body of Christ. If for instance God speaks to somebody's heart about starting a Bible school, once it is mentioned publicly, you can be sure five other people will start a Bible school right away. God did not speak to them, but they stole the word from you. Another instance is if God put it in your heart to build an orphanage and instead of praying about it and consulting with a spiritually matured person for help, you just start talking about it, then you find several other people who heard your vision start establishing orphanages.

Sometimes you even get discouraged by the number of orphanages that spring up so that you will not find it necessary to build what God instructed you to establish. You are robbed of what could have brought you glory. It is not wickedness to conceal a matter, it is part of your glory to keep some things private about your life and destiny.

I want you to know that there are stealers of the word, there are stealers of visions, and there are people who will steal God's plan for your life if you just go about sharing that. At times as a leader, you must learn how to be quiet. People may perceive you in several negative ways but then it is sometimes okay to be discreet about certain information. You must learn how to keep some information within an inner circle. Your profits can be marginalized, gains reduced to zero simply because your strategies are on the streets. Our competitors got hold of our strategies, took a clue from it and outwitted us. It is important to first execute your ideas and generate success before people get to discover your strategy. But then when you reveal how you intend to accomplish your goals ahead of execution, you have sold out your strategy to your competitors, lost and diminished your chances for overwhelming success. It is after you succeed that you can share with others, not when you have not even put the foundations down. When you see a person who is quiet, he is not necessarily foolish, rather, he may have learnt to keep things in his head.

"Now when they had seen Him, they made widely known the saying which was told them concerning this Child. And all those who heard it marveled at those things which were told them by the shepherds. But Mary kept all these things and pondered them in her heart"

Luke 2:17-19

The shepherds who were informed of the birth of Jesus by angels paid a visit to Jesus Christ lying in the manger and made known to Mary and Joseph what was told them concerning this child. You see they went talking about it, they were saying we have seen the savior. But notice verse 19, Mary did not go talking about saying that 'this baby I am carrying is the savior'. She never did. She never said the angel spoke to me so I know that what I have conceived is from the Holy Ghost. Prophets came and spoke over the baby but she just pondered them in her heart and kept the information. Be like Nehemiah and Mary the mother of Jesus Christ and learn how to keep things in your heart. If you have to talk about something, let it be the right time. Ask yourself this question several times, when you feel like saying something: "Lord is it the right time"? Be careful even with some fellow believers. God said I am against them, they may steal it, though I did not tell them because they have a habit of stealing it from one another. If you did not tell it they would not have known. Remember it is an honor to conceal a matter.

SECRETS – The Benefits of Being Discreet

Chapter Four

SEE THAT YOU TELL NO MAN

"Now after six days Jesus took Peter, James, and John, and led them up on a high mountain apart by themselves; and He was transfigured before them. His clothes became shining, exceedingly white, like snow, such as no launderer on earth can whiten them. And Elijah appeared to them with Moses, and they were talking with Jesus. Then Peter answered and said to Jesus, "Rabbi, it is good for us to be here; and let us make three tabernacles: one for You, one for Moses, and one for Elijah" - because he did not know what to say, for they were greatly afraid. And a cloud came and overshadowed them; and a voice came out of the cloud, saying, "This is My beloved Son. Hear Him!" Suddenly, when they had looked around, they saw no one anymore, but only Jesus with themselves. Now as they came down from the mountain, He commanded them that they should tell no one the things they had seen, till the Son of Man had risen from the dead. So they kept this word to themselves, questioning what the rising from the dead meant"

Mark 9:2-9

I n this story of the transfiguration, when Moses and Elijah appeared to the Lord Jesus Christ on that mountain, Peter requested for permission to make booths for Jesus, Moses and Elijah. Though it was a good idea, this was not God's plan or purpose for the meeting. Moses and Elijah came to talk to Jesus about his impending death in Jerusalem. Immediately after this experience, Jesus charged them saying "see to it that you tell no man of this until after my resurrection." In other words, 'do not speak too soon about this but keep this to yourself'. Then he provides the time frame "Until I am resurrected from the dead." In fact John and Peter could not talk about it until the resurrection of Jesus.

It is very important that in our dealings, to know when to say what and when not to say some things. Jesus did not tell them never to speak about it, but he said see to it that you tell no man of this until my resurrection. Keep this to yourself for now until I die and I have resurrected from the dead. In my opinion, the reason why the Lord might have said to keep this information to themselves, is because the Jews believed in Moses and Elijah as their glorified prophets. They did not know where Moses and Elijah were buried so the whole transfiguration story will have been murky and could potentially stir a lot of controversy. The Jews may have considered such a story anything but magical, cultic and demonic. It could lead to so many things that may potentially have derailed the agenda of the cross. They will have possibly stoned Jesus Christ prematurely. So it is important for us to understand that when the Lord is dealing with us on certain issues, we have to know that there are some things we cannot speak about until we get the clearance or go ahead from God.

"Now a leper came to Him, imploring Him, kneeling down to Him and saying to Him, "If You are willing, You can make me clean." Then Jesus, moved with compassion, stretched out *His* hand and touched him, and said to him, "I am willing; be cleansed." As soon as He had spoken, immediately the leprosy left him, and he was cleansed. And He strictly warned him and sent him away at once, and said to him, "See that you say nothing to anyone; but go your way, show yourself to the priest, and offer for your cleansing those things which Moses commanded, as a testimony to them." However, he went out and began to proclaim *it* freely, and to spread the matter, so that Jesus could no longer openly enter the city, but was outside in deserted places; and they came to Him from every direction"

Mark 1:40-45

In the above story where Jesus Christ has just performed an outstanding miracle in the life a man, we will think the right thing is for him to go out there and give a public testimony about what the Lord has done. But then after the man was healed, Jesus strictly charged him saying, "See that you say nothing to anyone; but go your way, show yourself to the priest, and offer for your cleansing those things which Moses commanded, as a testimony to them." In accordance with the Law of Moses, it was the priest who would certify your healing. The priests will have to examine you and give you a clean bill to that effect and then you can be integrated back into the society. Many of us may think; 'Well if it is the Lord who healed, how come the Lord does not want you tell anybody'. We know that is going to inspire people and encourage them to trust for a miracle but then God has a greater purpose for each miracle. In spite of the strict instruction from Jesus about being discreet, we know that this man did not obey the Lord. In fact, right away he began to publish the matter. He went everywhere telling everybody. This became a great hindrance to the ministry of Jesus, since he could no longer openly enter into the city. Whatever God had to be done for that city was hindered because this man went to say what he was commanded not to say. Think about that. As a result, Jesus had to stay in the wilderness and in desert places. Who knows what God's plan was for that city? God's plan for a city is greater than his plan for an individual. So an individual's blessing is not supposed to get in the way of the blessing for a city. But because this individual did not know how to keep his mouth shut, he hindered the whole city from receiving a greater blessing from the master.

Let us always think of the greater purposes of God. Always think of the greater purposes, not just the narrow perceptions that fit our mentality. At times we do a greater good by keeping our mouths shut than talking. Many people will testify that after testifying about certain good things, everything came to a standstill. This is the case because the testimony was given ahead of time. There is definitely a time for everything. It is important to ask the Lord if you should go ahead and talk about some things or to keep quiet about them.

At times God has a greater blessing for a family but premature exposure of information could hinder, delay and even abort the divine set up. At times God has a greater plan for your life as an individual but then you speak too soon. And I believe we all have to be wise to avoid certain hindrances and obstacles. We must be conscious of not triggering unnecessary envying and jealousies that arises in people's heart because they get a glimpse of what God has in store for us. Those who hear from our mouths the divine plan repeat it until the whole world get to know about it. Most often the truth becomes little and the exaggerated version prevails.

"But you, Daniel, shut up the words, and seal the book until the time of the end; many shall run to and fro, and knowledge shall increase"

Daniel 12:4

The book of Daniel is mostly a revelation given to a man called Daniel. After God had given him all this revelation he said shut it up, this is not the time to talk about it. Shut those revelations up and he showed him at what time the book will be opened, which was the time of the end. The fact that the Lord has said something to you and sent you does not mean you immediately go and publish it abroad. Just because God has shown you something that will come upon the nation does not mean you go about talking about it. God showed Joseph the plan for his life and he immediately went about to published it. We know the results that followed. We can spare ourselves a lot of battles and bitterness if we can follow the wisdom of God. The instruction; "See to it" becomes our responsibility. Do not say "I could not help it, I had to say it". You can help it. We must learn to keep God's secrets.

Chapter Five

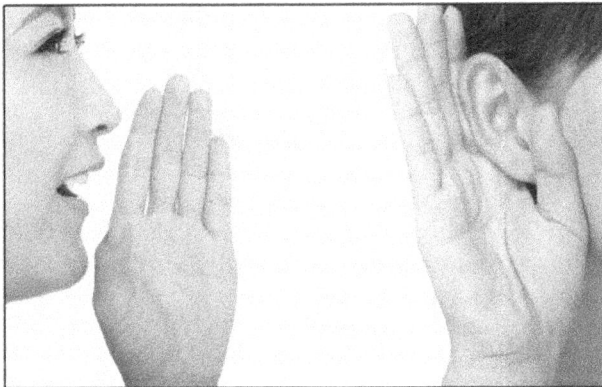

DO NOT BE A TALE BEARER

"You shall not go about as a talebearer among your people; nor shall you take a stand against the life of your neighbor: I am the Lord"

Leviticus 19:16

SECRETS – The Benefits of Being Discreet

An important law God gave to Israel through Moses was that no one of them should become a talebearer. A talebearer is one who goes about peddling unsolicited secrets. Such people have cultivated the habit of always having something to say. Today, technology has facilitated us with the telephone and the internet that makes it easier to access people regardless of distance. Talebearers do not necessarily go about anymore. They can be stationed at one place but still pass on a lot of information through the telephone and internet. In the early days when the telephone was not yet invented, you could be in your house and someone will come around and say; "I was just passing by and I decided to say hello". Or they could say; "I was passing by and I felt strongly to check on you". Then the next thing is "Have you heard?" Or "Are you aware?"

Most often, we think that talebearers only carry the tales of others. What we do not realize is that, in the process of providing you with the secrets of other people, they are paying attention to developments in your home as well as any information you might provide during the conversation. In short they carry your own tale as well to their next stop. It works both ways.

A talebearer is like an automated door that opens of its own accord once a person approaches it. Anytime they meet a human being, it is as though something is triggered in them to start divulging whatever others have told them in confidence. They just have to talk. Since some of the information may be incomplete they are forced to spice it up with what they do not know in order to make it credible and complete. The worst part of this is that when they are informing you of some secret and you even nod your head in agreement with what they say, at their next stop, they will add your nod to spice up their tale, so as to say; even you know that what they are saying is true. This new listener will say "I believe it." Guess what, at their next stop they will add the second listener to the tale and say, "he or she knows about it and also believes the story." Usually they end by saying; "Please do not tell anybody what I told you, I love you that is why I informed you about it."

There are others who have itchy ears and constantly want to know the business of others. Do not let anyone get any information from you. Your attitude should always be that, you are not going to get it from me. We have all made mistakes by telling people's secrets to others. It is not our responsibility to tell people the secrets of others. If you desire some information about a person, the right thing is to go to them yourself and ask directly. Do not try to know other people's secrets indirectly through third parties.

In order for God's dealing with us to be kept and preserved, then we got to be careful about talebearers. We ought not to be talebearers ourselves. If you want to carry good news, it should be the preaching of the gospel of salvation. Scripture says "How beautiful are the feet of those who carry good news... who announce peace and proclaim that our God reigns." Preaching the good news about the kingdom of heaven is different from tale bearing. Preaching is productive since it facilitates the spreading of the gospel of our Lord Jesus Christ and advances the kingdom of God. However some of us tell God's secrets and peddle them as though we are preaching the gospel. If God informs us of His intentions to punish a person or nation, we go about spreading it without His permission. As a result of such tale bearing some lives, families and Church communities have been destroyed. The ministry of a leader or a minister may be destroyed because people say things which ought not to be said.

"A talebearer reveals secrets: but he that is of a faithful spirit conceals the matter"

Proverbs 11:13

We all ought to develop faithfulness that is loyalty in our spirit. It is important that we cultivate loyalty to God. If God says something to us and not to others, it is because he wants to trust us with a secret. Wars have been started within nations and between nations because of what someone said. Ships have been sunk because of false information from people. Be careful of passing on information to someone who is a talkative or a talebearer. Communities and Churches get divided and destroyed as a result of tale bearing.

You know there are some people who are constantly whispering to others. Usually it is not so much what happened but the fact that people start talking about it. If there are just two talebearers in a community or church of perhaps a thousand people, you can be sure that this group will not stand the test of time. Sooner or later a crisis will emerge within the group that is a direct result of tale bearing. At times people may judge the outcome and say 'it is not the fault of the tale bearer, rather it is the people that did the wrong'. The question is who has not done wrong before? The church is not filled with people who are perfect, but imperfect. Whatever goes wrong can be fixed. But these people who go about fishing for information and peddling it about are the real trouble makers.

When unfaithful people begin to talk, it stirs up envy and jealousy in the heart of people and sparks them into action. It works in the home even among our children. We have to be careful what we say about one child to the other child. That can be very unhelpful. Many parents have caused dissention among their children because they said something about one child to the other. If as a parent, your child confides in you a deep secret, you must endeavor to keep it confidential.

Some leaders and ministers are talebearers. You cannot confide in them because they cannot restrain themselves from talking. I know some leaders and ministers who when they visit and you entertain them with a drink, you activate things in them. With just a glass of juice you activate their 'talk-activity'. Such people easily divulge information about others as well as leadership decisions that are not meant for the public. Talkative people always reveal secrets without knowing it. Most often it is difficult to trace who revealed a secret because it was not revealed intentionally. However too much talk, can make an innocent man a natural talebearer. Do not be an unsolicited informant. Develop the capacity to keep stuff in your heart for five years without talking about it. Pray for grace to preserve information in your heart.

Many people who function as intercessors have destroyed people's faith and Churches because of topics that came up in the prayer meeting. A prayer topic may become the basis for gossip and goes 'viral' so that everyone gets to know what they ought not to know. An intercessor must not be a talkative. The result of the mix of prayerfulness and too much talk results in tale bearing. The two does not go together. Some people suffer from a chronic diarrhea of words and it must be cured. All of us need help. God wants to do things with us but then He is watching our faithfulness with secrets.

I pray that this message will sink into your spirit and help you develop loyalty with information entrusted to you. A year or two years from now, you will look back and be happy you made this change in how you handle secrets. Determine very strongly that you will not be a tale bearer and also that you will not entertain a talebearer in the name of Jesus. Be on your guard to only entertain people who are of a faithful spirit, who can conceal a matter. God could trust Daniel with his secrets and you can also be trusted if you pray for the grace to become faithful.

SECRETS – The Benefits of Being Discreet

Chapter Six

KEEP YOUR LIFE BY
KEEPING YOUR MOUTH

"He that keeps his mouth keeps his life: but he that opens wide his lips shall have destruction"

Proverbs 13:3

The word 'keeps' appears twice in this scripture but they do not have the same function. One is when you shut or close your mouth and the other refers to life preservation. Here the scripture is saying that when you keep a secret, you actually protect your life. Think about it. What is your life? Everything that your life consists of; your health, your business, your education, your relationships and your marriage. Everything about you constitutes your life. Did you know that when you keep your mouth shut, you are protecting your life? If you will flourish in life, one of the greatest truths is that you must learn how to keep your mouth shut. No doubt the scripture says "study to be quiet." Twice Paul wrote to the Church in the book of Thessalonians, "study to be quiet and mind your own business." This is a truth directly embedded in God's word. If God said it, I am going to apply it to my life. "He that keeps his mouth, keeps his life." If you are going to build a hedge around your life and protect your wellbeing, too much talking has to be avoided.

People have lost their relationships because of careless talk. Nations have been destroyed, marriages broken and businesses have attracted strong competitors because of careless speaking. Some people have the attitude of, 'For me I will say it, I do not mind'. That is a wrong attitude. Keep your mouth shut. It is not everything you know that you should speak about. God has a hidden wisdom which is hidden from the enemy.

"However, we speak wisdom among those who are mature, yet not the wisdom of this age, nor of the rulers of this age, who are coming to nothing. But we speak the wisdom of God in a mystery, the hidden *wisdom* which God ordained before the ages for our glory, which none of the rulers of this age knew; for had they known, they would not have crucified the Lord of glory. But as it is written: "Eye has not seen, nor ear heard, Nor have entered into the heart of man The things which God has prepared for those who love Him." But God has revealed *them* to us through His Spirit. For the Spirit searches all things, yes, the deep things of God"

1 Corinthians 2:6-10

If the rulers of this world had known, they will not have crucified the Lord Jesus. He kept it away from them. He ordained it for our glory. God kept it to himself till the right time and now it is in manifestation. We do not know that much of the hindrances that have manifested in our lives is because of careless talk. We do not connect it, but the scripture is teaching us that we encounter so much opposition in certain areas of life because we talk too much. People mistakenly associate quietness with ignorance and weakness. It is better to look

SECRETS – The Benefits of Being Discreet

ignorant and weak than to suffer from a diarrhea of words. When you have the disease called diarrhea, every second you have to go to the restroom. Some people can never sit down for two to three hours without saying anything. They have to pick up the phone and call somebody. They got to say something.

When people realize that you suffer from a diarrhea of words, they often avoid you. If most of your friends are pulling away from you, it may be because you open your mouth too wide. They do not return your calls, though you leave them several messages. Our mouths go a long way to affect everything about us in life.

"Even a fool, when he holds his peace, is counted wise: and he that shuts his lips is esteemed a man of understanding"

Proverbs 17:27

A man and woman of knowledge do not talk too much, they use few words. When a person shuts his mouth and is quiet and observing, he is esteemed as a man of understanding. Do you want to build a hedge around your life? Please watch your mouth.

"And Joshua had commanded the people, saying, Ye shall not shout, nor make any noise with your voice, neither shall any word proceed out of your mouth, until the day I bid you shout; then shall ye shout"

Joshua 6:10

We have all heard of the story of how the wall of Jericho fell, but most often, preachers do not tell the entire details of it. We are only told the wall of Jericho fell because the Israelites shouted. But then shouting was just one out of the whole thing. Joshua commanded the people; "you shall shout" and did not suggest it to them. When we read on you will notice that it was on the seventh day that Joshua said when the trumpet sounds then you give a shout. Six days they went around the wall without saying a word, without making a noise. Think about that, for the walls of Jericho to fall we got to be silent for six days and talk one day. In the same way, for the walls that hinder us to fall, we have to do less talking. Many of us have it in reverse, often doing more talking than keeping quiet. In fact many of us talk for six days and we keep quiet for one day. That is not a strategy. He said six days of quiet and one day of talking. The more you talk the more you allow the walls of Jericho to remain standing. Six days Joshua said do not even make any noise. Do not let a word come out of your lips until I tell you otherwise. What a discipline. We got to understand this discipline. Six days they kept this in their heart. Can you keep information for a year and never talk about it, nor whisper about it? Victory comes to those who do less talking.

Finally it is important that we cultivate the virtue of being quieter and talk less. James 1:19 reads, "Let every man be swift to hear, slow to speak." This scripture is a great word of caution that can make us wise.

Chapter Seven

TRUE SPIRITUALITY

"If anyone among you thinks he is religious, and does not bridle his tongue but deceives his own heart, this one's religion is useless"

James 1:26

SECRETS – The Benefits of Being Discreet

T he Apostle James was writing to the twelve tribes that were scattered abroad who believed in the Lord Jesus Christ and He said, "If any man amongst you seem to be religious", that is seem to be spiritual. In view of our relationship with God it is appropriate to say spiritual. He continued, "and this person does not bridle his tongue". The second thing here is if the person does not tame his tongue then he deceives his own heart. Furthermore, this man's religion is useless or vain. If we cannot tame our tongue, it renders our spirituality as vain. The word vain here means devoid of power, success, no purpose and profitless. In other words spirituality can potentially bring great benefit to us because it has power within it. However if a person seems to be spiritual but cannot control the tongue, then the person's spirituality cannot afford the person any benefit which in essence suggests that other people are not also going to benefit.

To consider a person as truly spiritual, then the fundamental standard is the quality of control over the tongue. A person who has true spirituality is someone who is able to hold his tongue in check. In this light, we can confidently state that a talkative person is not spiritual at all. Naturally we know that one characteristic of children is that they talk too much, whilst the sign of a mature person is that they know when to speak and when not to speak. The

Apostle James is speaking to all of us and that is why he says "if anyone". He was quite burdened with how Christians used their tongue as he wrote again, "Be slow to speak and quick to hear." True spirituality is developed by curbing the tongue.

Controlling your tongue does not mean you should not talk to people. It is the character of knowing what to say at the right time and what not to say. We do not become spiritual for spirituality sake. It has to bring benefit to us otherwise that spirituality is useless.

The scriptures mention Samson as one of the judges who led Israel at some point. Over the years, the lessons to be learned from Samson's story have been really misinterpreted. The story about Samson reveals him as a unique personality who can be an analogy for a giant, a nation, a corporation or an individual that has been raised up to do great things. He was raised by God to deliver Israel. Though Samson was able to accomplish great feats of deliverance for Israel from Philistine oppression, his life was cut short and his ministry was not executed to the fullest extent that God intended. To understand how his leadership of Israel was terminated prematurely, we have to piece up carefully his life story. First of all, Samson's birth was announced to his parents by an angel.

"For behold, you shall conceive and bear a son. And no razor shall come upon his head, for the child shall be a Nazirite to God from the womb; and he shall begin to deliver Israel out of the hand of the Philistines"

Judges 13:5

"Now Samson went down to Timnah, and saw a woman in Timnah of the daughters of the Philistines. So he went up and told his father and mother, saying, "I have seen a woman in Timnah of the daughters of the Philistines; now therefore, get her for me as a wife. Then his father and mother said to him, "*Is there* no woman among the daughters of your brethren, or among all my people, that you must go and get a wife from the uncircumcised Philistines?" And Samson said to his father, "Get her for me, for she pleases me well." But his father and mother did not know that it was of the LORD—that He was seeking an occasion to move against the Philistines. For at that time the Philistines had dominion over Israel"

Judges 14:1-4

Samson saw a Philistine woman and immediately fell in love with her. This was a taboo as Israelites were forbidden to engage in marriage with people from other heathen nations. His parents tried to talk him out of it but then the scripture clearly states that

Samson's infatuation for this Philistine woman was orchestrated by God.

So though we generally assume that Samson's desire to marry the Philistine woman was wrong, it was actually from God. God had a purpose for this relationship in the scheme of the overall design of Samson's life and destiny. It was a divine setup through which God was seeking occasion against the Philistines. Obviously Samson's ministry was to bring him in constant engagement with the Philistines. Most of the great exploits he accomplished over the Philistines were always as a result of altercations involving his relationships with Philistine women. This gave him a reason to attack the Philistines and thereby weakening their dominion over Israel.

"Afterward it happened that he loved a woman in the Valley of Sorek, whose name *was* Delilah. And the lords of the Philistines came up to her and said to her, "Entice him, and find out where his great strength *lies,* and by what *means* we may overpower him, that we may bind him to afflict him; and every one of us will give you eleven hundred *pieces* of silver." So Delilah said to Samson, "Please tell me where your great strength *lies,* and with what you may be bound to afflict you." And Samson said to her, "If they bind me with seven fresh bowstrings, not yet dried, then I shall become weak, and be like any *other* man." So the lords of the Philistines brought up to her seven fresh bowstrings, not yet dried, and she bound him with them. Now *men were* lying in wait, staying with her in the room. And she said to him, "The Philistines *are* upon you, Samson!" But he broke the bowstrings as a strand of yarn breaks when it touches fire. So the secret of his strength was not known. Then Delilah said to Samson, "Look, you have mocked me and told me lies. Now, please tell me what you may be bound with." So he said to her, "If they bind me securely with new ropes that have never been used, then I shall become weak, and be like any *other* man." Therefore Delilah took new ropes and bound him with them, and said to him, "The Philistines *are* upon you, Samson!" And *men were* lying in wait, staying in the room. But he broke them off his arms like a thread. Delilah said to Samson, "Until now you have mocked me and told me lies. Tell me what you may be bound with." And he said to her, "If you weave the seven locks of my head into the web of the loom"— So she wove *it* tightly with the batten of the loom, and said to him, "The Philistines *are* upon you, Samson!" But he awoke from his sleep, and pulled out the batten and the web from the loom. Then she said to him, "How can you say, 'I love you,' when your heart *is* not with me? You have mocked me these three times, and have not told me where your great strength *lies.*" And it came to pass, when she pestered him daily with her words and pressed him, *so* that his soul was vexed to death, that he told her all his heart, and said to her, "No razor has ever come upon my head, for I *have been* a Nazirite to God from my mother's womb. If I am shaven, then my strength will leave me, and I shall become weak, and be like any *other* man." When Delilah saw that he had told her all his heart, she sent and called for the lords of the Philistines, saying, "Come up once more, for he has told me all his heart." So the lords of the Philistines came up to her and brought the money in their hand. Then she lulled him to sleep on her knees, and called for a man and had him shave off the seven locks of his head. Then she began to torment him, and his strength left him. And she said, "The Philistines *are* upon you, Samson!" So he awoke from his sleep, and said, "I will go out as before, at other times, and shake myself free!" But he did not know that the LORD had departed from him"

Judges 16:4-20

In all the exploits recorded of Samson in engagement with the Philistines, he conquers them as a lone soldier. He was an unbeatable one-man-army. Over and over again, he demonstrated supernatural power to defeat any number of Philistine warriors that pitched up against him. The Philistines were now frustrated with their failure to overcome this single force of defense for Israel. They now sought to know the secret of Samson's strength. They hired his lover Delilah with the promise of financial reward, if only she would find out the secret to Samson's strength. It was espionage, where people use cunning ways to access confidential information. Three times, he told Delilah something else apart from his secret and try as they did, he did not become weak. It is instructive to note that it was not a Philistine woman who brought him down rather it was Samson himself. I say this because true spirituality progresses and radiates in silence. It is in silence that victory comes rather than by much babbling.

When people see your success they want to know how you got there. The enemy always wants to know the secret of our success and this is what these Philistines were after, the secret. The fall of Samson was simply because he did not curb his tongue. In short, Samson was not very spiritual. Though his name is mentioned in the book of Hebrews as one of the heroes of faith, he had an issue with his tongue that led to his premature demise.

Be careful what you say to your friends. Just be quiet and only speak when you have something useful to say. This truth applies to nations and not to believers alone. People are paid to spy and find out information that will give them an advantage. Nations spy against themselves and we also have industrial espionage where businesses spy out the secrets of their competitors to position them strategically in an advantage. Three times, Samson did not tell Delilah the truth which led her to harass Samson until he finally let the secret out. The secret to Samson's supernatural power was announced by an Angel of God prior to his birth. It was not common information. This was how God intended Samson to conquer the Philistines and for a while Samson had operated in this unusual ability to suppress the Philistine oppression of Israel. However his lover Delilah became the hired spy of the Philistines. She harassed Samson until he was subdued. Delilah operated as a spirit of harassment. A mission which was announced by angels was prematurely aborted through espionage. Inability to protect the secret of his personal relationship with God cost him his life and purpose. He ended up blind, imprisoned and used as the grinding machine of the Philistines. Sometimes we think some friends love us so much that we tell them our secrets. It is important to be very cautious of nosy and inquisitive friends because such friends may turn to become our enemies and use such information against us. Do not let anyone push you to succumb and say those things that are fundamental to your success and strength.

Chapter Eight

LEARNING FROM OTHERS

There is an interesting story in the scriptures about a man of God who was given a divine assignment. He executed the assignment with the demonstration of signs and wonders but then his life was cut short by a tragic mistake of failure to be discreet with certain classified details of the mission.

"And behold, a man of God went from Judah to Bethel by the word of the LORD, and Jeroboam stood by the altar to burn incense. Then he cried out against the altar by the word of the LORD, and said, "O altar, altar! Thus says the LORD: 'Behold, a child, Josiah by name, shall be born to the house of David; and on you he shall sacrifice the priests of the high places who burn incense on you, and men's bones shall be burned on you.'" And he gave a sign the same day, saying, "This *is* the sign which the LORD has spoken: Surely the altar shall split apart, and the ashes on it shall be poured out." So it came to pass when King Jeroboam heard the saying of the man of God, who cried out against the altar in Bethel, that he stretched out his hand from the altar, saying, "Arrest him!" Then his hand, which he stretched out toward him, withered, so that he could not pull it back to himself. The altar also was split apart, and the ashes poured out from the altar, according to the sign which the man of God had given by the word of the LORD. Then the king answered and said to the man of God, "Please entreat the favor of the LORD your God, and pray for me, that my hand may be restored to me." So the man of God entreated the LORD, and the king's hand was restored to him, and became as before.

1 Kings 13:1-6

The prophet mentioned in this scripture is referred to as a man of God. He was God's man and could speak into the future. Clearly he was also endowed with the ability to demonstrate supernatural signs and wonders by the Spirit of God. He was sent by God to declare a judgment against the altar upon which the evil kings of Israel offered sacrifices to idols. At the time the prophet was delivering the judgment against the altar, King Jeroboam was offering sacrifice at this altar. The king was angry at the prophet and stretched out his hand pointing at the prophet with a command for his arrest. The hand of King Jeroboam kind of froze so that he could not pull it back again. The altar also split supernaturally to confirm the prophecy of the man of God. King Jeroboam entreated the prophet and the king's hand was restored. Without a shadow of doubt it was clear that this prophet was sent by God to deliver this message that was validated with signs and wonders.

"Then the king said to the man of God, "Come home with me and refresh yourself, and I will give you a reward." But the man of God said to the king, "If you were to give me half your house, I would not go in with you; nor would I eat bread nor drink water in this place. For so it was commanded me by the word of the LORD, saying, 'You shall not eat bread, nor drink water, nor return by the same way you came.'" So he went another way and did not return by the way he came to Bethel."

1 Kings 13:7-10

At this point of the story we see the test of his maturity as a man of God. The king is happy that his hand is healed by the prayer of the prophet and to express his gratitude he invites the prophet to the palace for a meal and a reward. The prophet should have given a simple answer of "NO" and head back to his own home. He had properly executed the mission for which God sent him. Unfortunately his immaturity set in when the king gave him a simple invitation that required a simple decline of "NO" based on God's instruction that was a part of how he was to execute the mission. He spoke too much and divulged information that was not to be made public. The prophet spoke to the hearing of all the people present and he said "If you were to give me half your house, I would not go in with you; nor would I eat bread nor drink water in this place. For so it was commanded me by the word of the LORD, saying, 'You shall not eat bread, nor drink water, nor return by the same way you came." He went beyond what he should have said. He should not have said God told me but rather keep the information to himself.

Even when God tells you to keep away from certain people, do not go about saying, "God said I should stay away from people like you". This will not make sense to the people you tell and they will label you as a lunatic or an extremist and take offense. In any case divulging such information to people will always hurt you and never help you. There are many things that God speaks to us about, which should never be told to anyone. Now let us read the consequence of divulging this information that the prophet should have kept to himself.

"Now an old prophet dwelt in Bethel, and his sons came and told him all the works that the man of God had done that day in Bethel; they also told their father the words which he had spoken to the king. And their father said to them, "Which way did he go?" For his sons had seen which way the man of God went who came from Judah. Then he said to his sons, "Saddle the donkey for me." So they saddled the donkey for him; and he rode on it, and went after the man of God, and found him sitting under an oak. Then he said to him, "*Are* you the man of God who came from Judah?"And he said, "I *am*." Then he said to him, "Come home with me and eat bread." And he said, "I cannot return with you nor go in with you; neither can I eat bread nor drink water with you in this place. For I have been told by the word of the LORD, 'You shall not eat bread nor drink water there, nor return by going the way you came.'" He said to him, "I too *am* a prophet as you *are,* and an angel spoke to me by the word of the LORD, saying, 'Bring him back with you to your house, that he may eat bread and drink water.'" (He was lying to him.) So he went back with him, and ate bread in his house, and drank water. Now it happened, as they sat at the table, that the word of the LORD came to the prophet who had brought him back; and he cried out to the man of God who came from Judah, saying, "Thus says the LORD: 'Because you have disobeyed the word of the LORD, and have not kept the commandment which the LORD your God commanded you, but you came back, ate bread, and drank water in the place of which *the LORD* said to you, "Eat no bread and drink no water," your corpse shall not come to the tomb of your fathers.'" So it was, after he had eaten bread and after he had drunk, that he saddled the donkey for him, the prophet whom he had brought back. When he was gone, a lion met him on the road and killed him. And his corpse was thrown on the road, and the donkey stood by it. The lion also stood by the corpse. And there, men passed by and saw the corpse thrown on the road, and the lion standing by the corpse. Then they went and told *it* in the city where the old prophet dwelt. Now when the prophet who had brought him back from the way heard *it,* he said, "It *is* the man of God who was disobedient to the word of the LORD. Therefore the LORD has delivered him to the lion, which has torn him and killed him, according to the word of the LORD which He spoke to him." And he spoke to his sons, saying, "Saddle the donkey for me." So they saddled *it.* Then he went and found his corpse thrown on the road, and the donkey and the lion standing by the corpse. The lion had not eaten the corpse nor torn the donkey. And the prophet took up the corpse of the man of God, laid it on the donkey, and brought it back. So the old prophet came to the city to mourn, and to bury him. Then he laid the corpse in his own tomb; and they mourned over him, *saying,* "Alas, my brother!" So it was, after he had buried him, that he spoke to his sons, saying, "When I am dead, then bury me in the tomb where the man of God *is* buried; lay my bones beside his bones. For the saying which he cried out by the word of the LORD against the altar in Bethel, and against all the shrines on the high places which *are* in the cities of Samaria, will surely come to pass." After this event Jeroboam did not turn from his evil way, but again he made priests from every class of people for the high places; whoever wished, he consecrated him, and he became *one* of the priests of the high places. And this thing was the sin of the house of Jeroboam, so as to exterminate and destroy *it* from the face of the earth"

1 Kings 13:11-34

There was an old scheming prophet whose sons had witnessed what the prophet had said and also the signs and wonders that had validated his message. The old prophet's sons told their father all the works the prophet had done and also the words he had spoken to the king. This old prophet was probably burnt out and was no longer significant and probably had diminished influence at this point in his life. When he heard about the notable deeds of this young prophet, it was an opportunity to revive his own significance and influence as a prophet. He gathered as much information from his sons and saddled his donkey in pursuit of this young prophet. He eventually caught up with the young prophet who had stopped to rest under a tree. The old prophet lied to the young man of God. With the words he heard from his sons, the old prophet concocted a message which he claimed he had received from God. Unfortunately the young man of God fell for this tale of deceit and followed the old prophet home to eat. While they were eating the old prophet was suddenly genuinely inspired of God to prophecy that because the young prophet had disobeyed the instructions of his mission, he will meet his demise by an attack of a lion. On his way home the young prophet was killed by a lion according to the prophecy of the old prophet. Though this young prophet had perfectly executed his divine

SECRETS – The Benefits of Being Discreet

assignment, because he could not bridle his tongue, he was slain by a lion.

As a man of God, you should not seek validation from the people you speak the word of God to. Is not the mailman paid to just deliver the mail without knowing what is in the mail? The word comes through me but it is not for me. If the word comes from the Lord, receive the word in faith and give praise to God because the things of God are received by faith. Trust in the Lord and do not try to figure out the word of God.

There is another story in the scriptures about a king by name Saul. The process by which he was anointed to become king of Israel provides lessons of prudence which we will be blessed to employ in how we handle certain information.

"There was a man of Benjamin whose name *was* Kish the son of Abiel, the son of Zeror, the son of Bechorath, the son of Aphiah, a Benjamite, a mighty man of power. And he had a choice and handsome son whose name *was* Saul. *There was* not a more handsome person than he among the children of Israel. From his shoulders upward *he was* taller than any of the people. Now the donkeys of Kish, Saul's father, were lost. And Kish said to his son Saul, "Please take one of the servants with you, and arise, go and look for the donkeys." So he passed through the mountains of Ephraim and through the land of Shalisha, but they did not find *them*. Then they passed through the land of Shaalim, and *they were* not *there*. Then he passed through the land of the Benjamites, but they did not find *them*.⁵ When they had come to the land of Zuph, Saul said to his servant who *was* with him, "Come, let us return, lest my father cease *caring* about the donkeys and become worried about us." And he said to him, "Look now, *there is* in this city a man of God, and *he is* an honorable man; all that he says surely comes to pass. So let us go there; perhaps he can show us the way that we should go." Then Saul said to his servant, "But look, *if* we go, what shall we bring the man? For the bread in our vessels is all gone, and *there is* no present to bring to the man of God. What do we have?" And the servant answered Saul again and said, "Look, I have here at hand one-fourth of a shekel of silver. I will give *that* to the man of God, to tell us our way." (Formerly in Israel, when a man went to inquire of God, he spoke thus: "Come, let us go to the seer"; for *he who is* now *called* a prophet was formerly called a seer.) Then Saul said to his servant, "Well said; come, let us go." So they went to the city where the man of God *was*. As they went up the hill to the city, they met some young women going out to draw water, and said to them, "Is the seer here?" And they answered them and said, "Yes, there he is, just ahead of you. Hurry now; for today he came to this city, because there is a sacrifice of the people today on the high place. As soon as you come into the city, you will surely find him before he goes up to the high place to eat. For the people will not eat until he comes, because he must bless the sacrifice; afterward those who are invited will eat. Now therefore, go up, for about this time you will find him." So they went up to the city. As they were coming into the city, there was Samuel, coming out toward them on his way up to the high place.[15] Now the LORD had told Samuel in his ear the day before Saul came, saying, "Tomorrow about this time I will send you a man from the land of Benjamin, and you shall anoint him commander over My people Israel, that he may save My people from the hand of the Philistines; for I have looked upon My people, because their cry has come to Me." So when Samuel saw Saul, the LORD said to him, "There he is, the man of whom I spoke to you. This one shall reign over My people." Then Saul drew near to Samuel in the gate, and said, "Please tell me, where *is* the seer's house?" Samuel answered Saul and said, "I *am* the seer. Go up before me to the high place, for you shall eat with me today; and tomorrow I will let you go and will tell you all that *is* in your heart. But as for your donkeys that were lost three days ago, do not be anxious about them, for they have been found. And on whom *is* all the desire of Israel? *Is it* not on you and on all your father's house?" And Saul answered and said, "*Am* I not a Benjamite, of the smallest of the tribes of Israel, and my family the least of all the families of the tribe of Benjamin? Why then do you speak like this to me?" Now Samuel took Saul and his servant and brought them into the hall, and had them sit in the place of honor among those who were invited; there *were* about thirty persons. And Samuel said to the cook, "Bring the portion which I gave you, of which I said to you, 'Set it apart.'" So the cook took up the thigh with its upper part and set *it* before Saul. And *Samuel* said, "Here it is, what was kept back. *It* was set apart for you. Eat; for until this time it has been kept for you, since I said I invited the people." So Saul ate with Samuel that day. When they had come down from the high place into the city, *Samuel* spoke with Saul on the top of the house. They arose early; and it was about the dawning of the day that Samuel called to Saul on the top of the house, saying, "Get up, that I may send you on your way." And Saul arose, and both of them went outside, he and Samuel. As they were going down to the outskirts of the city, Samuel said to Saul, "Tell the servant to go on ahead of us." And he went on. "But you stand here awhile, that I may announce to you the word of God"

1 Samuel 9

At times God gives us information of what will take place before it happens. It is possible for one to know certain things six months, one year or ten years before it happens. God had told Samuel the day before that Saul was going to come looking for him. Samuel the prophet kept this in his heart. In order to set up a meeting between Prophet Samuel and Saul, God used the donkeys that were lost to bring Saul out of the house. When the two met, Samuel chose the atmosphere in which to begin to disclose systematically God's message to Saul. First of all he set up a feast where Saul was seated in a prominent position. Secondly, Samuel instructed the cook to serve Saul with the special portion that was reserved for leaders. In this way Samuel was gradually unveiling the message from God to Saul through signs that would not be apparent to those present but then provide clues to Saul that something unusual was about to take place in his life.

Samuel demonstrated that he was a matured man of God by employing the spirit of wisdom to execute the divine assignment. To announce God's message to Saul, Samuel the prophet went with Saul to the top of the house. He had to excuse the servant because the message was not for the servant. Just because you are a prophet does not mean you must say everything in plain sight. For instance, you do not tell someone he has cancer in public. They may receive it better if this was done in private. The supernatural ability to reveal things that pertain to the future must never be done as a show off of one's prophetic prowess. The revelation gifts of the Holy Spirit are intended to bring profit and not pain. It is to facilitate to reposition ourselves to gain advantage and not intended to make us victims of gossip. Just as the prophet Samuel was discreet in how he presented the message of Saul's coronation to him, we have to be circumspect when carrying the word of God across to other people. There is a public and private ministry of the prophetic and we need to know when to use each one. It is sad to note that a lot of Prophets today do not operate in wisdom so they do more harm than good with their flamboyant methods of delivering prophetic messages.

"Then Saul's uncle said to him and his servant, "Where did you go?"So he said, "To look for the donkeys. When we saw that *they were* nowhere *to be found,* we went to Samuel." And Saul's uncle said, "Tell me, please, what Samuel said to you." So Saul said to his uncle, "He told us plainly that the donkeys had been found." But about the matter of the kingdom, he did not tell him what Samuel had said"

1 Samuel 10:14-16

There were several signs that Samuel told Saul will manifest to confirm the anointing that had come upon him. While on the way home, these signs came to pass, one of which included Saul prophesying with a band of prophets he was to meet. Saul's meeting with Samuel the prophet and the public sign of prophesying with the band of prophets was now public knowledge. When Saul returned home, his uncle asked him what the prophet had told him. The scripture says Saul did not tell him what Samuel had said to him. That information was not for his uncle to know.

"Do not curse the king, even in your thought; Do not curse the rich, even in your bedroom; For a bird of the air may carry your voice, And a bird in flight may tell the matter"

Ecclesiastes 10:20

A pastor friend of mine travelled overseas and brought me a gift of a very nice leather briefcase. Instead of thanking and praising God, I showed it to my friends and told them it was our mutual friend that had bought me this leather briefcase. These friends went to this man and started accusing him of buying me a briefcase and not buying any for them. They accused him of loving me more than them. Is it not a pity that I almost put this friend of mine into trouble with these people? I should have just kept the information to myself. Sometimes the things we say may hinder people from being a blessing to us.

There are many things we say to people innocently that ends up hurting our relationships with others. Though we cannot absolutely control how our words are conveyed or how they are understood by others, it is important that we give careful thought to our words, so that we can defend ourselves against any misrepresentation if questioned.

AFTERWORD

You have read this book
Your eyes have received light
Wisdom has been established in your heart
Your life has been deeply impacted
Now go and act on this knowledge

ABOUT THE AUTHOR

Affectionately called 'Rabbi', William Obeng-Darko is a gifted and an outstanding Bible Teacher. God has graced him with a strong Apostolic calling and an unction upon his life in the areas of Church organization, raising structures in Christian Ministries and Churches, founding Bible Schools, training believers for Christian service and has been involved in pioneering over thirty churches.

He has authored two books: Victory over Curses and Understanding the Prophet Movement. Rev. William's missionary outreach spans over twenty five years to cities, towns and villages in Africa, the former Soviet Union, United Kingdom, Netherlands, the Caribbean and the United States of America.

Pastor William is the founder of Open Door Missionary Church, a Bible believing charismatic church in Maryland and an Apostolic Teacher to the Body of Christ. He is married to his lovely wife Dr. Evelyn, who has been a very loving wife, partner in ministry and a strong supporter of his God-given dreams and aspirations. They are blessed with three children-William, David and Jasmine.

For information call:
800-455-2380 extension 802

Email:
info@pure-word.org

Or visit website:
www.purewordministries.org

* 9 7 8 1 9 4 0 2 6 0 0 1 3 *